The
Loman Family
Picnic

The Loman Family Picnic

by

Donald Margulies

GARDEN CITY, NEW YORK

Photos by Martha Swope.

Design by Maria Chiarino

ISBN: 1-56865-097-3

Manufactured in the United States of America

For
Charlene & Bob
and Howie

THE LOMAN FAMILY PICNIC was first presented at the Manhattan Theatre Club City Center Stage II (Lynne Meadow, Artistic Director; Barry Grove, Managing Director; Jonathan Alper, Series Director) in New York City, on June 6, 1989. It was directed by Barnet Kellman; the set design was by G.W. Mercier; the costume design was by Jess Goldstein; the lighting was designed by Debra J. Kletter; the music was by David Shire; the choreography was by Mary Jane Houdina; the sound was by Aural Fixation and the production stage manager was Renée Lutz. The cast was as follows:

DORIS . . . . Marcia Jean Kurtz
MITCHELL . . . . .Michael Miceli
STEWIE   . . . . .Judd Trichter
HERBIE   . . . . .Larry Block
MARSHA   . . . . .Wendy Makkena

THE LOMAN FAMILY PICNIC was subsequently produced (with changes in the text that appear in this volume) by Manhattan Theatre Club City Center Stage I, in November, 1993. It was directed by Lynne Meadow; the set design was by Santo Loquasto; the costume design was by Rita Ryack; the lighting was designed by Peter Kaczorowski; original music was by David Shire; the sound design was by Otts Munderloh; the choreography was by Marcia Milgrom Dodge; the fight director was Rick Sordelet and the production stage manager was William Joseph Barnes. The cast was as follows:

DORIS . . . . Christine Baranski
MITCHELL . . . . . . Jonathan Charles Kaplan
STEWIE   . . . . Harry Barandes
HERBIE   . . . . Peter Friedman
MARSHA   . . . . Liz Larsen

CHARACTERS

DORIS, 38
HERBIE, 40
MITCHELL, 11
STEWIE, 13
MARSHA, 23

TIME

Around 1965.

PLACE

Coney Island, Brooklyn, N.Y.

The
Loman Family
Picnic

ACT
ONE

Scene One

In the black: A Broadway overture segues into music like Mantovani's rendition of "Autumn Leaves."

At rise: A high-rise apartment in Coney Island, Brooklyn. Around 1965. A picture window looks out onto an identical, parallel high-rise building with dozens of picture windows. The room is decorated with Spanish Provincial furnishings: wrought-iron sconces, heavily carved wooden shelves, floor lamps, sofa, loveseat, TV/hi-fi console, etc. A door in the dining area leads to a terrace overlooking the neighboring building. It's after three o'clock on a late October afternoon. DORIS, *38 years old, wearing a housecoat over her pajamas, sits on the sofa with her wedding dress on her lap. She is cutting it to shreds with a pair of scissors.*

DORIS (*to us*): On the day I was married the world showed every sign of coming to an end. It rained—no, poured. Thunder. Cracks of lightning. Big Pearl S. Buck tidal waves. You get the picture. Did I turn back? Did I cancel? Did I say never mind, no thank you? A good omen, my mother told me. There had never been such a terrifying convergence of weather post-Noah; a good omen. Hail, did I mention hail? Like my mother's matzo balls falling from the sky shouting *Don't! Don't!* each time a knaidel smacked the roof of the rented limo. A better omen still, my mother said, hail. "What about sunshine, Momma?" I asked, "what about a sunny wedding day?" Also a good omen, my mother

3

said. (*A beat*) I began to distrust her. (*A beat*) Two seconds in my wedding dress: splattered with mud. I should've known. Look at this: ruined. From day one. (*Points to various stains*) Mud, rain, hail, locusts, boredom, moraine . . . (*Looking directly at us*) I love the way my life has turned out. I have two wonderful boys. Mitchell is my baby. He's eleven. And Stewie is gonna be bar mitzvahed next Saturday at ten in the morning, to be followed by a gala affair starring me. What boys I have! I'm very lucky, knock on formica. Smart?! Mitchell has a reading level, goes off the charts. So smart are my boys. Their father is not at all threatened by how smart they are. They aren't showoffs. I don't like showoffs. I raised my boys to stand out but not too much, you know? Otherwise people won't like you anymore. Look what happened to the Jews in Europe. Better you should have friends and be popular, than be showy and alone. My Aunt Marsha may she rest in peace taught me that. She was very popular. (*A beat. Refers to the wedding dress*) Last night was my wedding anniversary. Eighteen years. Herbie had to work, what else is new. I love the way my life has turned out. Did I say that already? On the day I was married the world showed every sign of coming to an end . . . (Mitchell, *11 years old, enters through the front door carrying schoolbooks*) Mitchell. What are you doing home from school?

MITCHELL: School let out; the day is over; I came home. It's 3:30.

DORIS: Oh, my God. You're home from school and I haven't been out all day? I didn't even put on any clothes? I'm not depressed.

MITCHELL: I didn't say you were depressed. What are you doing with your wedding gown?

DORIS: I got the greatest idea for a Halloween costume— you're gonna love this: The Bride of Frankenstein.

MITCHELL: You're gonna tear up your wedding gown for a costume?

DORIS: I'm not disenchanted with my marriage.

MITCHELL: I didn't say you were disenchanted with your marriage.

DORIS: I still love your father.

MITCHELL: I didn't say you didn't.

DORIS: I love my life. I love the way my life has turned out. Your father doesn't bore me. What if your father and I got a divorce? Who would you live with? Never mind, only kidding. So, how was school today?

MITCHELL: I owe Miss Schoenberg 50 cents for lunch. You forgot to put lunch in my lunchbox again.

DORIS: Did I? Oh, honey, I'm sorry. I'm not a negligent mother.

MITCHELL: I didn't say you were. I said you forgot. Anyone could forget.

DORIS: I guess I was just preoccupied with how much I love my life. Don't you love this room? Isn't it unusual? I need a job. I have to get out of the house.

MITCHELL: I have good news.

DORIS (*voraciously*): Ooo, what? I'd love some good news!

MITCHELL: Remember that poster I made for Brotherhood Week?

DORIS: The rabbi and the priest and the black hand shaking hands with the white hand?, yeah . . . ?

MITCHELL: Well, today Miss Schoenberg announced to the class that I was a city-wide finalist.

DORIS (*shrieks in delight*): OH, MY GODDD!! To the class?!!

MITCHELL: Yeah, and it's gonna hang in the bank!

DORIS: The bank?!

MITCHELL: The Lincoln Savings Bank.

DORIS: The Lincoln Savings Bank?! It's gonna *hang* there?

MITCHELL: Uh huh.

DORIS: With your *name?!*

MITCHELL: Yeah, on an index card or something, written.

DORIS: People are gonna see your *name?* In the *bank?*

MITCHELL (*proud*): Yeah.

DORIS: I'm dying. Sweetheart! Oh, this is wonderful news! I'm so proud of you! The bank! For everyone to see! You're talking finalist now, not the winner, right?

MITCHELL: Finalist, you know, like in Miss America before they choose the winner.

DORIS: So you're not the winner yet but you have a shot.

MITCHELL: Right.

DORIS: City-wide?

MITCHELL: Yeah. The winner gets to go to City Hall and meet Mayor Lindsay.

DORIS: I'm dying.

MITCHELL: The *Daily News* comes.

DORIS: Pictures?! With Mayor Lindsay?! Oh, God, what would I wear?

MITCHELL (*reminding her*): I'm only a finalist so far.

DORIS: That's right, you may not even win, I'm jumping the gun. Oh, sweetheart, you've made my day.

MITCHELL: Miss Schoenberg says I'm very creative, I could have quite a career as an artist.

DORIS: Well, I'm sure. *Both* my sons are very talented. And your father is not in the least bit threatened by you *or* your brother.

MITCHELL: Miss Schoenberg says I can do whatever I like when I grow up. I have so many options because I'm such a strong student. She says I shouldn't rule out the Ivy League.

DORIS: For what.

MITCHELL: For college.

DORIS: You're eleven years old.

MITCHELL: So? Miss Schoenberg says attitudes toward academic achievement are developed at a very early age. You've seen my report cards: I'm a born overachiever.

DORIS: You mean Harvard, Princeton?

MITCHELL: Yale . . .

DORIS: Tell Miss Schoenberg *she* can put you through college.

MITCHELL: She says there are scholarships.

DORIS: Look, sweetheart, we are not Ivy League. We are City College. We're not like those people. City College was invented for people like us. You get a perfectly decent education.

MITCHELL: Whatever happened to the immigrant ideal of education or death?

DORIS: It died in the Depression. Miss Schoenberg is a troublemaker.

MITCHELL: Don't you want me to fulfill my potential? Don't you want me to continue getting excellents?

DORIS: Of course I do. But don't let your head get too big, it's unseemly. To be excellent is one thing; to be outstanding is another. We aren't fancy people, we're hand to mouth. We are middle-middle class, smack in the middle.

MITCHELL: But, Mom—

DORIS: Do you want to kill your father completely? He's half-dead just treading water. How would we explain

Ivy League to the relatives? They think we're rich already, because we live in this luxurious high–rise; then they'd *really* despise us. We want everyone to love us. Remember what my Aunt Marsha always said may she rest in peace: Don't go around thinking you're better than everyone else 'cause you'll be alone in the end. Dream, my son, but not too big. (STEWIE, *almost 13, stomps through the front door*)

STEWIE: I've had it. Cancel the bar mitzvah.

MITCHELL: Hi, Stewie.

DORIS: What are you talking about cancel the bar mitzvah?! I can't cancel the bar mitzvah. What happened?

MITCHELL: Hi.

STEWIE: Mr. Shlosh is a cretin.

DORIS: He's a rabbi.

STEWIE: I don't *care* he's a rabbi, he's still a cretin. We're going over my Haftarah . . .

DORIS: Yeah . . .

STEWIE: I know almost all of it by heart.

DORIS: Thank God.

STEWIE: And I'm really singing it this time. Like Jerry Vale. Soft and sweet? It's so beautiful I'm embarrassing myself, I feel my cheeks getting hot. And I get through the whole thing perfectly, I sound just like the record, and he doesn't even compliment me!

DORIS: All right, so he's not gushy.

STEWIE: He's not *human.* (MITCHELL *laughs*) I decided to have a conversation with him?

MITCHELL: Yeah . . . ?

STEWIE: Big mistake. I mean, I've been sitting in this room with this guy with bad breath for years, reading the same stuff over and over, preparing me for the big day, right?, and he never even *talked* to me! I don't mean Talmudic dialogue, I mean your basic chat.

DORIS: What do you want from him?! He's an old man!

STEWIE: I gave up my *boyhood* to him, Ma! Hundreds of afternoons I'll never get back! I missed years of watching *You Don't Say* after school! That's irreplaceable, Ma.

DORIS: Oh, stop.

STEWIE: So I thought I was entitled to ask a *question* at least. I said to Shlosh, "Okay, so finally I can read all these little symbols right to left. Great. Now tell me

11

what it means." Well, the guy looks like he's gonna go berserk. (*To* MITCHELL) Like Ray Milland in *X: The Man With the X-Ray Eyes* right before he plucks his eyes out? (MITCHELL *giggles*) "Tell me what I'm *reading*," I said, "tell me what the words mean." He looks at me like I'm not speaking any known language. "What does it *mean?!*" I said, "what am I *say*ing?!" "What does it matter?" he says, "you can *read* it." "Yeah, but what does it *mean?!*" "It means you will be bar mitzvah!" he says. "But the words don't *mean* anything to me, they're just funny, *chuchy* little sounds." "Those funny sounds," he says, "are what make a boy different from a Jew!" "So?! You taught me how to *read* but you didn't teach me how to *understand!* What kind of Jew is that?!" This does not go over big. His lips are turning blue. I think he's gonna have an angina attack. (*Beat*) All *he* cares about is rolling out bar mitzvah boys to repopulate the earth. We *look* the part and we can sing, but we don't know what we're saying! I have had it!

DORIS: You have to go through with your bar mitzvah, Stewie.

STEWIE: You don't know what it's like, Ma, day after day of this. I'm being brainwashed.

DORIS: You're just getting cold feet. You'll be fine.

STEWIE: I can't do it, Ma.

DORIS: Yes you can. Just like Sammy Davis, Jr. Say it: yes I can.

STEWIE: Ma . . .

DORIS: He lost an eye and everything. And that man is a Jew. Yes I can, yes I can . . .

STEWIE: But I don't want to.

DORIS (*infuriated, through gritted teeth*): How *dare* you do this to me!

STEWIE (*his teeth are also gritted*): What? What am I doing to you?!

DORIS: You know how hard I've been working to make you a beautiful party?!

STEWIE: Me? It's not for me. *Make* your beautiful party! I just won't be there. Tell everybody I got the runs!

DORIS: Don't do this to me, Stewie! Don't make me cancel! We'll lose all our deposits! Is that what you want?! Hm?! Your father's blood money down the drain?! The hall, the band, the flowers?! The caterers?! I already bought my dress, what do you want me to do with it? Hock it? I've spent *days* laying out response cards like solitaire and clipping tables together! This is no time to be a prima donna, Stewie. One more week. That's all I ask. Give me the *nachas*, then you can do whatever the hell you want. You want to renounce Judaism, renounce Judaism. Become a monk, I don't care. (*A beat*)

STEWIE (*teeth gritted again*): Remember, Ma, I'm doing this for you. I'll go through with it, and sing nice, and make you proud, and make the relatives cry, but once I'm bar mitzvahed, that's it, Ma, I'm never stepping foot in that place. Never again.

DORIS: Thank you, darling, thank you. (*She kisses and tickles* STEWIE; *he squeals with delight*)

MITCHELL (*during the above*): Stewie? Hey, Stewie.

STEWIE (*annoyed*): What.

MITCHELL: You know the poster I made?

STEWIE: Yeah . . .

MITCHELL: I'm a finalist.

STEWIE (*unenthused*): Wow.

DORIS (*to us*): Isn't it wonderful how my boys get along?

(*Blackout.*)

14

Scene Two

Around midnight. Some lights are still on in the windows across the way. DORIS, STEWIE *and* MITCHELL *have all fallen asleep in front of the TV.* STEWIE *is lying flat on his back with his accordion strapped on. We hear a key in the front door and in a moment* HERBIE, *a burly 40-year-old, enters wearily, a shopping bag in each hand and newspapers tucked under his arm.*

HERBIE: Daddy's home! The provider is here! (*He waits, expecting to be greeted ceremoniously, but his sleeping family doesn't budge. Facetiously*) Gee, it's good to be back in my family's waiting arms! In the bosom of my family! Don't all of you jump up and kiss me at once! (*A beat*) Daddy's home! Another day, another dollar! (*A beat*) The warrior is back! I'm black and blue but I'm back in one piece! From a whole day of busting my balls for you! Gee, I can't wait to get up at six a.m. so they can be pounded to bits all over again! Oh, but look what Daddy brought! Wow! What a guy! What a Dad! (*Unloads as he speaks*) Milk, orange juice, half a dozen bagels: poppy, salt, cinnamon-raisin, pumpernickel, plain, garlic; one of each! Plus, for the boys: half gallon of their favorite, fudge swirl! Wow! Gee, thanks, Dad! Aw, you're welcome, son! (*A beat; still no reaction*) What a day! The place was a madhouse! Customers on the phone, at the counter! They were all over me! The cash register didn't stop! I still hear ringing in my ears!

15

I was so busy, I didn't even have time to pee! A whole day! I wouldn't be surprised if my bladder just *exploded* one of these days, *pshhhoo!*, like a water balloon! (*Takes off his shoes*) Phew! Can you believe a stink like that comes out of a man?! (*Massages his feet*)

DORIS (*stirs, sniffs his aroma*): Herbie? When'd you get home?

HERBIE: Hours ago.

DORIS: You did not. . . . Boys? Boys, wake up. (MITCHELL *yawns, rubs his eyes, etc.* STEWIE *remains asleep*)

MITCHELL: What time is it?

DORIS: Daddy's home; you're on.

MITCHELL: I have to get up for school soon. I need nine or ten hours in order to function properly.

DORIS: Just say hello to your father.

MITCHELL: Hi, Dad.

DORIS: Kiss him. (MITCHELL *sleepily gets up, kisses him*) STEWIE, play him that piece on the accordion. Stewie! (STEWIE, *still lying on his back, plays a song like "Lady of Spain" on the accordion. Banging is heard from downstairs as* STEWIE *rushes through the piece*) Isn't it wonderful how your son serenades you? You're not threat-

16

ened by Stewie's musical abilities, are you, Herbie? Of course not. (*Nudging* MITCHELL) Tell your father what happened in school today.

MITCHELL: What.

DORIS: You know, the big news. The bank, Mayor Lindsay.

MITCHELL: Oh, do I have to?

DORIS: Yes you have to. (*To* HERBIE) I'll go get your supper. (*As she goes off to the kitchen*) Wait till you hear *this* . . . (*Pause*)

HERBIE: Well?

MITCHELL: It's nothing. Can I please go to bed?

DORIS (*off*): No. Tell him!

MITCHELL (*sighs, then wearily*): Remember that poster I made?

HERBIE: Poster?

MITCHELL: I made a poster. (HERBIE *shrugs*) Remember she made me show it to you one night when you came home? (HERBIE *thinks, shrugs*) The rabbi? The priest? The black hand shaking hands with the white hand?

HERBIE: Oh, yeah. That was a poster?

MITCHELL: Yes.

HERBIE: Oh, okay. So?

MITCHELL: Today I found out I'm a finalist for the city-wide Brotherhood Week poster competition. (*A beat*)

HERBIE: A what?

DORIS (*off*): A finalist. City-wide. A contest.

HERBIE: Finalist?

DORIS (*off*): It means it was one of the best. In the whole city.

HERBIE: Is that good?

DORIS (*off*): Yes, it's very good.

HERBIE: Oh. Well, good.

DORIS (*off*): Tell him about Mayor Lindsay.

HERBIE: What about Mayor Lindsay?

MITCHELL (*dully, while yawning*): If I win, I get to meet Mayor Lindsay.

HERBIE: Oh. (*A beat*) I didn't vote for him. (MITCHELL *and* HERBIE *look at one another*)

DORIS (*enters with a plate of food*): Isn't it wonderful how your father takes pride in your achievements? Most fathers don't do that. Most fathers only know how to compete with their sons and are threatened by everything they do. You're very lucky. (*To* HERBIE) Here, I made you a dietetic dinner. Three-and-a-half ounce can of tuna packed in water with one tablespoon of low-calorie Miracle Whip in lieu of mayo. One scoop of low-fat cottage cheese on a bed of lettuce. I weighed and measured everything very carefully, according to Jean Nidetch. (*Sits down at the table with him; silence*) So? How was your day? (HERBIE *shrugs. Pause*) Business?

HERBIE (*shrugs, then*): Good.

DORIS: Uh huh. (*Pause*) Everybody?

HERBIE (*shrugs, then*): Same.

DORIS: Uh huh. (*She sighs; her boredom and despair are palpable but she continues to sit in silence, struggling to stay awake while watching him eat. There's a shift in the lighting and they're now convivially relating to one another, as old friends, stories they've never before shared, each telling how the other died*)

HERBIE: It was around eleven one night.

DORIS: Yeah . . . ?

HERBIE: We were in bed, watching the news. You got up to go to the john; I dozed off; you came back. The toilet was still running. And then you shook, like.

DORIS: Hm.

HERBIE: The kind of shake you do when you're in a dream, falling?

DORIS: Uh huh . . . ?

HERBIE: Well, your shake woke me up and I looked at you and you looked funny to me.

DORIS: Uh-oh.

HERBIE: Very white; and I touched you and you felt funny.

DORIS: Uy.

HERBIE: I shook you: Doris, Doris. It was like you passed out, only worse.

DORIS: Uy uy uy.

HERBIE: 9-1-1 I called. I held your cold foot and told you, we're gonna get you some oxygen, Doris, everything's gonna be okay. And the sirens came soon, red lights flashed 'round the windows, and the buzzer buzzed and I buzzed 'em in. They're on their way up, Doris, don't worry, any minute. . . . The bell. I let 'em in, I was still in my shorts and didn't even care, didn't even think to put on my pants. And they came in, noisy with oxygen, stretcher; they *zetzed* some furniture on the way in.

DORIS: Not my *furniture* . . .

HERBIE: Easy, I said, and led 'em to the bedroom, and I sat up in bed watching them work on you. Boy, they hit you hard.

DORIS: They did?

HERBIE: Don't hurt her, you got to do that so hard? They pumped on you, your pajama top was open, and I wasn't even embarrassed 'cause these guys are professionals, I thought, they do this all the time. Remember the time the car died on that bad part of Ocean Avenue and the Triple-A guys started her right up?

DORIS: Yeah . . . ?

HERBIE: That's what I thought: Come on, guys, start her up.

DORIS (*laughs affectionately*): Oh, Herbie . . .

HERBIE: Let's go. One more press, two more, come on DORIS, three more, come on, okay this time, *this* time, come on baby. You were gonna snap out of it like when you think in the movies somebody drowned but they cough up water and they're fine. Cough, Doris. Come on, cough. And then you were gonna sit up and turn pink again and say what the hell happened, Herbie?

DORIS: Of course.

HERBIE: I waited. (*A beat*) What the hell happened you were supposed to say. (*Pause;* DORIS *is shaking her head*)

DORIS (*after a beat*): Well, *you.* You took forever.

HERBIE: Yeah . . . ?

DORIS: Talk about milking it: longest deathbed scene in history.

HERBIE: You're kidding.

DORIS: The waiting. The drama. The boredom. What a character; couldn't let go. (HERBIE *laughs*) I thought I myself would die of exposure to weeks of fluorescent lighting and hospital food.

HERBIE: You're funny.

DORIS: Every day was something else. Good news one minute, talk about safe–deposit boxes the next. You did not know what hit you, my darling.

HERBIE: Is that so.

DORIS: You looked at me with a look: what is going on? Your lungs went, then your kidneys conked out and the whites of your eyes went yellow and you blew up like Buddha.

HERBIE: Geez . . .

DORIS: You were all tubes and bags of plasma and shit, bubeleh, and your big belly trembled with the air the machine fed you. "Do you want to die?" I asked you on Day 12, and you shook your head yes.

HERBIE: I did?

DORIS: Yes, and then something remarkable happened to your face.

HERBIE: What.

DORIS: It lost all the tensed-up lines in your forehead and round your mouth. And your features looked young and smooth, like when you were a G.I. You were Claude Rains turning visible again, for the last time, before my very eyes. The old Herbie came back, the *young* Herbie, the Herbie before *everything, my* Herbie, smooth of brow and cute of nose. . . . The face of my oldest of friends came into focus out of the fog of machines and sour odors. . . . I got you back for a second, Herbie, so letting you go wasn't so bad. (HERBIE *holds her hand. They look at one another for a beat. He remembers something*)

HERBIE: Oh, and the part I thought you'd love—

DORIS: What.

HERBIE: While they were pumping away at you?

DORIS: Uh huh . . . ?

HERBIE: The doorbell rang. The schmuck from downstairs.

DORIS: Friedberg?

HERBIE: The schmuck, right?

DORIS: Yeah. What did *he* want?

HERBIE: Wait. "What the hell kind of racket's going on up here," he says, "you know what time it is?!!" "Look," I said, "my wife just passed away."

DORIS (*amused*): Uy vey.

HERBIE: "Oh yeah?" the schmuck says, "oh yeah? Well you should hear what it sounds like downstairs!" (DORIS *and* HERBIE *laugh hysterically. Pause. The lights shift back to present reality.* DORIS *yawns*)

DORIS: I give up. Mitchell, do me a favor: keep your father company while he eats, I can't keep my eyes open. (MITCHELL *takes her place at the table*)

24

HERBIE (*to* MITCHELL; *looking at his dinner with distaste*): You want this?

DORIS: You see how much he loves you? Good night, boys. (*She taps* STEWIE *as she exits to her bedroom.* STEWIE *groggily gets up off the floor, the accordion bellows sounding, and goes to his room. Silence.* MITCHELL *yawns, taps his foot, while looking through the newspaper*)

HERBIE: You want to go out, throw a football around?

MITCHELL: Now?

HERBIE: That was a joke.

MITCHELL: We've never thrown a football around in our lives.

HERBIE: I know; that's the funny part.

MITCHELL (*after a pause, he steps away from the table and speaks to us*): For school, Miss Schoenberg made us read this play that Arthur Miller wrote a long time ago, before I was born, about this salesman with two sons who lives in Brooklyn? Sound familiar? I know; I read it like three times 'cause I couldn't believe it either. There are all these similarities. Except Willy Loman, the guy in the play?, the salesman?, doesn't sell lighting fixtures. (*Beat*) Anyway, in the play he goes insane and kills himself by smashing up his car so his family can collect his insurance money, even though I thought you can't collect if you commit suicide, which is what I said in class but Miss Schoenberg said not necessarily. (*Beat*) Arthur Miller himself grew up in this very same spot practically. Many years ago. He walked the same streets I walk every day. He played in our schoolyard probably. I heard that his family's house was one of the houses they wrecked so they could build our middle-income luxury building here in Coney Island. At least that's what Miss Schoenberg said. (*Beat*) Anyway, we have to get up in front of the class and do like oral book reports? But instead of doing the usual if-you-want-to-know-how-he-kills-himself-you-have-to-read-the-play kind of thing, I decided I'm gonna do something else, something different. (*Beat*) So, I'm writing this musical-comedy version of *Death of a Salesman* called *Willy!* With an exclamation point. You know, like *Fiorello!*? *Oklahoma! Oliver!*? So far I've come up with a couple of songs. Like, when Biff and Happy are up in their room and they hear Willy downstairs talking to himself? They sing this song called "Dad's a Little Weird" which goes: (*Sings*) "Dad's a little weird, he's in a daze. Could it be he's going nuts, or is it just a phase?" (*Beat*) Well, it's a start. What do you think?

(*Blackout.*)

Scene Three

The middle of the night. The apartment is dark. Most of the windows in the building across the way are dark, too. DORIS *has insomnia; she wanders into the living room smoking a cigarette. We hear, off in the bedroom,* HERBIE *snoring.*

DORIS (*through gritted teeth, to herself*): That snoring . . . if he doesn't stop that snoring . . . it rips at my *kishkas* every time he breathes. Every time he breathes is one more tear in my life. I love my life I love my life I love my—(*To us*) We have to stay together, at least till after the bar mitzvah. What would be the point? I have to have my day of glory. We have to be intact. Otherwise it's bittersweet forced-smiles brave-front stuff. "This is Mrs. Norman Maine." Destroys me every time. When it was on the Million Dollar Movie three times a day for a week, W.O.R. Channel 9, I turned on the TV the last five minutes for a guaranteed cry. "Hello, everybody. . . . This is . . . Mrs. . . . Norman . . . Maine." I'm getting misty just thinking about it. And she'd bring the house down. Everybody'd jump to their feet for a standing ovation, clapping till their hands hurt. Fifteen times a week I bawled in front of the TV. The boys'd come in from school, take one look at me pink-faced and teary and say, "Uh-oh; *Star is Born*," and go off to their room. (*A beat*) Now, if Herbie walked into the waves at Coney Island. . . . If he walked into the ocean à la James Mason and made me a widow, there's no question I'd go through with the bar mitzvah. I'd wear black sequins and clutch my boys to me with my head held high like Jackie Kennedy in the rotunda. *Then* I'd go through with it solo. But a divorce? (*During the above, a woman is seen climbing down onto the terrace from the one above. She is dressed in '40s attire, a brunette beauty with her hair in a pageboy. Her name is* MARSHA *and she's 23 years old. She looks in the picture window, opens the terrace door and steps inside*)

MARSHA: *There* you are, Doll.

DORIS: Aunt Marsha.

MARSHA: I been looking all over for you. All these apartments look alike. I almost dropped in on the Glucksterns by mistake.

DORIS: Come in. What do you think of my life? What do you think of little Doris now? Hm? (MARSHA *explores the room*) What you had to say always meant so much to me. What do you think? Does it look the way you once imagined my life would look when you held me in your arms, like a big sister at a pajama party, and we dreamed out loud together? Hm, Aunt Marsha?

MARSHA (*after a beat*): *Spanish,* Doll?

DORIS: No? It's so unusual, don't you think? I go for Spanish. I don't know what it is about Spanish. Maybe it has something to do with the Inquisition. It's a taste I cultivated on my own. You don't like it.

MARSHA: Who said?

DORIS: I always thought you'd approve; isn't that funny? You're always looking over my shoulder whenever I go shopping. To this very day: what would Aunt Marsha think? I see you nod or make that face. (MARSHA *jokingly makes a disapproving face*) Yeah, that's it. You never liked it when I went too fancy. Not too fancy, you don't want to be too fancy. You taught me that.

MARSHA: You funny kid.

DORIS: Kid? I'm thirty-eight years old, Marsh. You'd've hated thirty-eight. Sometimes I think you had the right idea.

MARSHA: What, checking out?

DORIS: Stopping time. For you time is stopped; for the rest of us it goes on and on but you stay young. You're dead now longer than I knew you. Longer than I knew you and not a day goes by—

MARSHA: So show me your dress for the bar mitzvah.

DORIS: I'm afraid now.

MARSHA: *Show* me.

DORIS (*starts to go*): You're not gonna like it.

MARSHA: Shut your trap; let me see.

DORIS: Well . . . (*She goes and returns with the dress*)

MARSHA: Oh, Doll . . .

DORIS: I don't know, I thought the color . . .

MARSHA: It's *you*.

DORIS: Yeah?

MARSHA (*holds the dress against* DORIS): Oh, yeah, that's swell!

DORIS: Really? You don't think the color maybe—

MARSHA: Are you kidding, I love it.

DORIS: Oh, Marsh. . . . You don't know how many shops. . . . Finally, on Kings Highway. . . . You really like it?

MARSHA: I'm knocked–out.

DORIS: I knew you *would* be. When I bought it, I said to myself—It's so good to see you.

MARSHA: You think I would miss your kid's bar mitzvah?

DORIS (*a beat; getting something off her chest*): I gotta tell ya, Marsh: I don't want you to get the wrong idea. I have *two* boys, you know.

MARSHA (*pleased*): Doll! *Two?*

DORIS: Mitchell I named for you. I would've named my first after you but I was holding out for a girl.

MARSHA: Makes sense. Thanks, kid. (MARSHA *continues exploring the room;* DORIS *watches her*)

DORIS: You still got the greatest legs in the world.

MARSHA: That's me, Betty Grable. (*Looking out the window*) How high up are we, I lost count.

DORIS: Ten stories, ten luxurious stories up in the air and thirteen on top of that. This is modern luxury.

MARSHA: Well, Doll, to tell you the truth . . . I had in mind for you a place with *trees.*

DORIS: There are trees, way down there. See? They're little stick trees 'cause they were just planted, but they're still trees. One day their trunks'll be big and thick. Everything's *new*, Marsh. Clean and new. We're the first. We moved in and the walls were white and the rooms still smelled of paint.

MARSHA: Whatever makes you happy.

DORIS: You should've seen the place we lived *before*. I don't know how we did it. A slum; the neighborhood was going to hell. But *here!* Hot water always. Rec room. Elevators that work. Security patrolled by German shepherds. A Waldbaum's that delivers. This is a big step up for us. *Luxury*, I'm *telling* you. Like fancy people. I hope not *too* fancy.

MARSHA: To think this is Brooklyn . . .

DORIS: Oh, we worked hard for all this, Marsh, you don't know. This is progress. I love our high–rise ghetto. *Look* out there. I can't wait for Hanukkah; Hanukkah looks like Kristalnacht here: a bonfire of orange–flame menorah bulbs burning in thousands of windows. A brick wall of electric flame! We're not alone. You know how good that feels? They moved us up, closer to heaven. Jews upon Jews who are glad to be here, who came as far as we did, from Flatbush, from Williamsburg, from East New York. Jews who escaped the Nazis, who escaped their relatives, who fled the *schvartzes*. Millions of miles of wall–to–wall carpeting that, if placed end to end, would reach from here to Jupiter and back. Instead of stoops they built us these little terraces. Sometimes I have to restrain myself from doing the cha–cha over the edge just to see what it would feel like going down. (*A beat; a confession*) I hung my last sconce today. I'm done decorating, Marsh. I bought my last *tschatchke*. My life is over.

MARSHA: Hey, don't talk like that.

DORIS: It is. My life is over, Marsh.

MARSHA: I'm not gonna sit here and listen to you talking like some sad sack. Now, I don't know about you, but I want to have some fun! (*Pulls* DORIS *to her feet*)

DORIS (*protests girlishly*): Marsh. . . . What are you doing?

MARSHA: Come on, I'm not gonna take no for an answer . . .

DORIS: I don't believe you! (MARSHA *leads* DORIS *in a swing step and hums/sings an upbeat '40s number, something like "Shakin' the Blues Away."* DORIS's *ambivalence subsides and, laughing, throws herself into the dance. Soon,* MITCHELL *appears in his pajamas, roused by the sounds. He watches for a moment*)

MITCHELL: Mom?

DORIS (*stops dancing*): Mitchell! Sweetheart! Come here, there's somebody I want you to meet. (*To* MARSHA.) This is my baby, Mitchell.

MARSHA: Oh!

MITCHELL (*going to her*): Mommy, it's the middle of the night.

DORIS: Mitchell, do you know who this is?

MITCHELL (*shyly*): No.

DORIS: This is my Aunt Marsha.

MITCHELL (*recognizing her*): Oh, yeah.

MARSHA: Hello, handsome.

MITCHELL: Hello. You look like your picture.

MARSHA (*charmed*): I do? So, you know who I am?

MITCHELL: Uh huh.

MARSHA: I was your grandma's baby sister.

MITCHELL: I know. You were only like eight years older than my mother. Like a big sister to her. She talks about you all the time.

MARSHA: Oh, yeah?

DORIS: See? It's true, I talk about you constantly.

MARSHA: What does she say?

MITCHELL: I don't know. She tells us how nice and beautiful you were and everything.

34

MARSHA: Oh, yeah? What else?

MITCHELL: How popular you were. And how being popular is one of the most important things in life 'cause otherwise you'll be alone. And, also how you really knew how to have a good time.

MARSHA: She told you all that, huh.

DORIS: Isn't he something? Doesn't forget a thing.

MARSHA: And what else did she tell you?

MITCHELL: Oh, yeah: How when you were twenty-three you slipped in the shower and got a concussion and died.

MARSHA (*beat*): Is that what she told you?

DORIS: Well . . .

MITCHELL: Yeah, so now I'm extra careful when I take a shower 'cause I don't want to slip in the bathtub and die like you.

DORIS (*a beat*): Mitchell, honey, why don't you go back to bed? You have to get up for school in the morning. Say goodnight to Aunt Marsha.

MITCHELL: Goodnight, Aunt Marsha.

MARSHA: Goodnight.

MITCHELL: Nice meeting you, finally.

MARSHA: Nice meeting you, too, handsome. (*He waves and goes back to bed. Pause*) What did you tell them?

DORIS: What do you mean?

MARSHA: You told your boys I slipped in the shower? Is that what you told them?

DORIS: What was I supposed to tell them?! They're children! (*Pause*) Oh, Marsh, I just tried to keep the good stuff alive.

MARSHA: Oh, yeah, sure. Sure you did, Doll. You did. We were pals, you and me; great pals.

DORIS: You ruined me, Marsh.

MARSHA: Just myself. I ruined myself.

DORIS: And me. You took a part of me with you I never got back, never.

MARSHA (*a beat*): Yeah? Did I do that? Sorry, kid. I didn't mean it. I wasn't thinking, you know? I thought I was indestructible. Who doesn't when they're my age? I took a trip to the wrong side of the tracks and got lost there, accidentally on purpose. The wrong side has its

36

moments, you know, depends on where you're standing. I liked the parties. And the booze. I liked watching my Yiddishe Momma rip hair from her head.

DORIS: Poor Bubba.

MARSHA: I loved the men. Oh, the men. I ruined *myself,* kiddo. Nobody did me in but me. I didn't mean to take no casualties.

DORIS: I had to be the good girl for the both of us. I did all the right things. You missed my wedding, Marsh. You're eighteen years late. I love my life, Marsh, I love the way my life has turned out. Don't you love this room? Isn't it unusual? I want you to be proud of me. I love my life I love my life. . . .

MARSHA: Shhh . . . (MARSHA *gently rocks* DORIS *as the lights fade to black.*)

Scene Four

An alarm clock sounds during the blackout. The light of dawn illuminates a scrim through which we see the suggestion of MITCHELL *and* STEWIE's *room.* STEWIE *is in the top half of a bunk bed.* MITCHELL, *in his pajamas, stands at the edge of the scrim looking in the living room at* HERBIE, *who sits perfectly still, staring onto space. Dressing for work, he's got one sock on and holds the other.*

MITCHELL (*whispers, to* STEWIE): He's staring again. (STEWIE, *in the top bunk, grunts*) Stewie, he's staring again.

STEWIE: What time is it?

MITCHELL: Look . . .

STEWIE: What *time* is it?

MITCHELL: Six something.

STEWIE: Six something?!

MITCHELL: One sock on, one sock off.

STEWIE: It's not even light out.

MITCHELL: Every morning now.

STEWIE: We could've slept another *hour* . . .

HERBIE (*to himself; trying to recall*): What did I dream?

MITCHELL (*overlap; to* STEWIE): Shhh. He's talking.

STEWIE: To who?

MITCHELL: No one.

STEWIE: Oh, great.

HERBIE (*still musing out loud*): I know I dreamed *something* . . .

STEWIE: Why do you get up for this?

MITCHELL: I don't know . . .

HERBIE: . . . Maybe not . . .

STEWIE: You *know* he's crazy . . .

MITCHELL: Yeah . . .

STEWIE: Why do you have to wake me up all the time?

MITCHELL (*genuinely*): I'm sorry . . . I thought you were interested . . . (*He begins dressing for school*)

HERBIE (*to us*): Maybe I don't have dreams anymore. I mean I must, but I don't remember. I don't remember a thing. My childhood? The war? Show me a picture of me taken someplace and I couldn't tell you where. I won't remember the name of the buddy I had my arm around. Ask me what year my kids were born, I couldn't tell you. Either of them. I know I was married eighteen years ago 'cause that's what Doris told me; the other night was our anniversary. I know how old I am; I'm forty years old. I was born in '25, but the exact date they're not sure, and the midwife who signed the birth certificate put my sex down as female. So I don't know; I don't know. I remember Dame May Whitty was in

The Lady Vanishes . . . but I don't remember my father even shaking my hand.

STEWIE (*to* MITCHELL): He's crazy. Let's face it. He's gone. Lost in action.

HERBIE (*to us*): Did *my* father throw *me* a bar mitzvah? I don't even remember *being* bar mitzvahed. If I *was* you can be sure nobody thought twice about it. They say we were very poor when I was young. (*Shrugs*) I don't remember. Supposedly we were on relief. Six kids in three rooms. No doors. No privacy. Hand–me–downs from my brothers. . . . Nothing ever started with me, it ended with me. I didn't have much; that much I remember. You stop *wanting,* so what you don't *have* doesn't matter. This is the Depression I'm talking about. I got through those years with my eyes shut tight and holding my breath like when you're under water. Got the hell outta *there,* straight to the Army. War was an improvement. Then I met Doris, then I married her, got this job, kids. . . . And I go through every day with my eyes shut tight and holding my breath, till the day is over and I can come home. To what? What kind of home is left to come home to by the time I come home?

MITCHELL (*to* STEWIE): What's he thinking when he seems to be thinking?

STEWIE: Hm?

HERBIE (*shrugs; to us, but responding to* MITCHELL'*s query*): I don't know; nothing. I'm thinking I don't know what to say. I'm thinking if I *do* say something, I hope it's not stupid, the wrong thing to say.

MITCHELL (*to* STEWIE): Was he always like this? Did he ever have anything to say?

HERBIE (*to us; as before*): It seems to me, in the days when I *would* say what was on my mind, I'd be shot down an awful lot. The more shot down you get, the less likely you are to say what's on your mind.

MITCHELL: What would that be like?

HERBIE (*to us*): It kills you after a while, thinking all the time how . . . (*A beat*) You don't even pay attention what's being said anymore 'cause you're too busy worrying how you might come off.

MITCHELL (*sighs*): Boy . . . (*He gathers his schoolbooks*)

HERBIE (*to us*): So I shut up a long time ago. It was a decision I made after something happened, something I don't remember what. I remember deciding well, fuck–'em–all one day, and Doris has handled it ever since. I let her do the talking. What the hell, I save my breath.

STEWIE (*to* MITCHELL): Where you going?

MITCHELL: In.

STEWIE: Well. . . . Might as well practice . . . (STEWIE *picks up his Haftarah book and sings softly through the rest of the scene*)

HERBIE (*to us*): I'm still waiting for her, for somebody, to notice and ask: What's up, Herbie? We'll all drop dead first. (MITCHELL, *schoolbooks in hand, tentatively enters the living room.* HERBIE *senses his presence and looks up and sees him. Pause*)

MITCHELL (*in explanation*): Cereal. (*Pause. They continue to look at one another*)

HERBIE (*finally*): That's *good.* It's *good* you eat breakfast. (*A beat.* MITCHELL *nods, starts for the kitchen, but stops*)

MITCHELL: Um . . . Dad?

HERBIE (*turns; expectantly*): Yeah, son? (*A beat.* MITCHELL *shakes his head "nothing," shrugs and exits to the kitchen.* HERBIE *watches him go. We hear* STEWIE *practicing his Hebrew as* HERBIE *finishes dressing. Light fade to black.*)

Scene Five

In the black: A Broadway show tune like "The Pajama Game" is playing on the hi–fi.

At rise: MITCHELL, *singing along with the music (he knows every word by heart), stands by the hi–fi as he puts on a skeleton costume. Soon,* STEWIE, *dressed as a hunchback with a stocking over his face distorting his features, sneaks up on him. He does a good Charles Laughton imitation. He attacks* MITCHELL *and knocks into the console, causing the needle to skid across the record.*

STEWIE: "Sanctuary! Sanctuary!" (STEWIE *gets* MITCHELL *in a headlock. The two roughhouse for a while*)

MITCHELL: Let me go.

STEWIE: "Sanctuary!" (*More roughhousing*)

MITCHELL (*no longer enjoying himself*): Let me go!! Stewie!! Stop it!! (*Etc.*) (*Their play degenerates into a real fight;* STEWIE *knocks* MITCHELL *to the ground and sits on him*)

DORIS (*off*): I hear body–drops in there!! (*The fight ends as abruptly as it began*)

STEWIE (*calls to* DORIS): Let's go already!!

DORIS (*off*): I'm not ready yet!

STEWIE (*to* DORIS): I don't want to wait!

DORIS (*off*): You will wait for your mother!! I gave you

life!! (HERBIE *enters through the front door and doesn't bat an eye at his sons' costumes*)

HERBIE: Daddy's home! (*Unpacks milk and orange juice*)

MITCHELL: Hi, Dad.

STEWIE: Hi, Dad. (*Calls*) Ma! He's home!

DORIS (*off*): Herbie?

HERBIE: It's my early night. Doesn't anybody remember my early night? I should've gone out to a movie or something. I could have a chippie on the side, no one would know the difference.

DORIS (*off*): I remembered, I remembered . . . (*Pause*)

HERBIE (*to the boys*): So? What's new? (*They shrug*) Any good news to tell me?

MITCHELL: No.

STEWIE: No.

HERBIE: No good news? Gee . . . I count on you guys . . . (*A beat; to* STEWIE) Let me guess. Some sort of holiday, right?

STEWIE: Right.

44

HERBIE: Halloween I bet, right?

STEWIE: You got it, Dad.

HERBIE (*to* MITCHELL): You, I can tell what *you* are. (*To* STEWIE) Who *you* supposed to be?

STEWIE (*mumbles in exasperation*): The Hunchbackanotredame.

HERBIE: The what?

STEWIE (*enunciating carefully*): The Hunchback of Notre Dame.

HERBIE: Oh, yeah. So you're gonna go trick–or–treating, hm?

MITCHELL: Yeah.

STEWIE (*loudly*): We're waiting for Mommy.

DORIS (*off*): Shut up in there, Stewart.

HERBIE: Your mother's going trick–or–treating? (*Calls*) You're going trick–or–treating, Doris?

DORIS (*off*): So?

HERBIE: So nothing.

STEWIE (*calls*): Hurry up, Ma! I'm suffocating under here!

DORIS (*off*): So take off the stocking!

HERBIE: Take off the thing, you won't suffocate! (STEWIE *stares at him for a beat, then silently exits. Another beat*) Hey, Mitch. Wanna see something?

MITCHELL: What.

HERBIE: Come here. (MITCHELL *approaches.* HERBIE *takes a business card out of his pocket and hands it to him*)

MITCHELL: What's this.

HERBIE: What's it *say*.

MITCHELL (*reads*): "Fred Werner, Regional Supervisor, Southwest, House and Home Stores, Incorporated." (*Looks up at* HERBIE) So?

HERBIE: Guy comes into the place. Out–of–town guy in a suit. 'Bout my age. Tall. Looks like Robert Young.

MITCHELL: Yeah, so.

HERBIE: Comes up to me. "Can I help you?" I say. "Looking for anything in particular? Bathroom, kitchen, dining room; fluorescent, chandelier, poles." My usual shpiel. I'm feeling good. I just had my chicken salad

46

sandwich to go, and a Patio diet cola; I was just break-
ing into an orange, my fruit with lunch.

MITCHELL: Yeah . . . ?

HERBIE: The guy is there, talking to me, asking me *this*
fixture, *that* fixture. I'm rattling off model numbers: You
mean the B624? Comes in silver finish and also brass.
Plated. K455? I'm afraid we're out of stock. "Are you
the manager here?" he asks me. "Why, yes I am, the
fixture showroom is my domain. I laid out the showroom with all the fixtures *on* so you can see what they
look like. I believe you got to see what a fixture looks
like *lit* 'cause that's how you're gonna use it; a light is
meant to be *on,* giving off *light.*" The guy is very im-
pressed with my ideas. The thing is you never know
who you're talking to, son; remember that in all walks
of life. Guy could be a guy who runs a chain of restaurants nationwide; if he likes my style, my approach, I
could land an order in the thousands. You never know
who you're talking to and that's a fact.

MITCHELL: Uh huh.

HERBIE: So, he says to me, the guy, "You really seem to
know your stuff, Herb." And the fact is I do, I don't
have to snow him. I been in home improvement my
entire life, I tell him. Well, since after the war. I say
"war," turns out to be the magic word, sets off a whole
other thing, and half an hour goes by, we're talking.
That's when he hands me his card.

MITCHELL: Okay, so.

HERBIE: You heard me talk about House and Home, right?

MITCHELL: I *think* . . .

HERBIE: They're the biggest. They're all over the country. They're putting guys like my boss out of business. Well. This guy—(*Takes back the card to look at the name*) Fred—wants me to manage—are you ready for this?— they've got four stores in and around Albuquerque—

MITCHELL: Albuquerque, New *Mexico?!*

HERBIE: Wait. And he wants me to manage all four lighting showrooms.

STEWIE (*who's been listening from afar all along*): New Mexico?!

HERBIE: Is that a compliment or what? You see what he thinks of your dad? That's a big responsibility.

MITCHELL: Well, yeah. Congratulations.

STEWIE: Ugh. Are we moving to New *Mexico?*

HERBIE: I didn't say yes, I said I would think about it.

STEWIE (*calls*): Ma, Daddy wants us to move to New Mexico.

48

HERBIE: I didn't say that, I said I would think about it.

DORIS (*off; overlap*): Not New Mexico. There are no Jewish people in New Mexico.

HERBIE (*calls*): This guy Fred Werner says the climate's gorgeous, year round.

DORIS (*off*): Werner? That's a German name, Werner. There are Indians in New Mexico. And Germans.

HERBIE (*calls*): But isn't it nice that he wants me?

DORIS (*off*): We just furnished, Herbie. We're throwing a bar mitzvah. We have *people* here, our people are *here*.

HERBIE (*calls*): But isn't it nice he wants me to think about it?

DORIS (*off*): Very nice. (DORIS *enters dressed in her tattered wedding gown, her hair teased wildly, her face monstrous with makeup. She presents herself with a flourish, laughing madly*) Ta dahhh!! (*The boys love it and clamor around her*)

STEWIE: Ma! Wow!

MITCHELL: You look great! Boy, everybody's gonna flip!

DORIS (*to us*): I'm telling you, this is inspired. I'll go around with the boys to all the neighbors and they won't know who I am. They'll think I'm just another crazy kid out trick–or–treating. People always mistake me for their older sister, that's how young I look. When I take the boys to the movies, the matron makes us sit in the children's section; I don't even bother to argue. I was married young. Eighteen. Well, twenty. I'm not obsessed with age. (*To* HERBIE) Would you've recognized me on the street? I bet not. (HERBIE *is hurt, incredulous; a beat*)

HERBIE: You tore up your dress?

DORIS: I'm surprised you noticed. I ripped it good.

HERBIE: You tore up your *wedding* dress?

DORIS (*after a beat; meaning, I shouldn't have?*): No?

HERBIE: Your *wedding* dress?

DORIS: It was old; it was faded.

HERBIE: So you tear it up?

DORIS: It was ruined from day one. Remember the rain—?

HERBIE: How could you do it?

DORIS (*after a long pause*): How? Why. (*Meaning, why do you ask?*)

HERBIE: You could just tear it up?

DORIS: It's a joke! A gag!

HERBIE: A gag?

DORIS: It's Halloween, Herbie, what's the matter with you?

HERBIE: You were married in that dress.

DORIS: But it's so old–fashioned now.

HERBIE: We were married, that's what you wore.

DORIS: A long time ago. Look how faded. It was white once. Remember the mud—?

HERBIE: This is a joke to you?

DORIS: No? (*Pause*) What is the big deal? It's not like I have a daughter to—

HERBIE: How do you do that?

DORIS: What?

HERBIE: The dress you wore to your wedding. It's supposed to mean so much. How does a girl rip up—

DORIS: I was never gonna wear it again. It was getting old and faded hanging at the back of my closet eighteen years; what's the matter with you?! All of a sudden you're gonna take it personal? "The Bride of Franken-stein." (*As she goes to the kitchen*) God, HERBIE, where's your sense of humor? (*Returns with three shopping bags and hands one to each of the boys*) Here, boys, bags for your loot. Remember, no eating till we check for razor blades.

STEWIE (*à la Quasimodo*): "Sanctuary! Sanctuary!" (STEWIE *goes, followed by* MITCHELL *who walks backwards, his eye on his parents*)

DORIS (*to* MITCHELL): Go ahead. Wait for me at the elevator. We'll go up to twenty-three and work our way down. How's that?

MITCHELL: Okay. (*He puts on his skeleton mask but lingers in the doorway, watching*)

DORIS (*to* HERBIE; *meaning the dress*): The thing still fits me, how do you like that? (*A beat*) Pulls a little bit 'cross the back, I had to use a safety pin, but not bad considering I had two kids. You can't tell, can you? (HERBIE *shakes his head; a beat*)

HERBIE: Go ahead. The boys are waiting. (*A beat*)

DORIS: I made you a tuna plate. It's in the fridge.

HERBIE: Good. (*A beat*)

DORIS: We won't be back late. (HERBIE *shrugs, "I don't care." They look at one another for a long time, then*) Sing to me "Autumn Leaves."

HERBIE: What?

DORIS: Sing to me—(STEWIE *appears at the front door, pushing* MITCHELL *aside*)

STEWIE: Ma-a. . . . (STEWIE *goes, but* MITCHELL *stays in the doorway*)

DORIS (*calls, while still looking at* HERBIE): I'm coming. (*She starts to go, stops; a beat*) You were kidding about New Mexico. Right?

HERBIE: Sure.

DORIS: That's what I thought. See ya later. (DORIS *steers* MITCHELL *out, exits.* HERBIE *is alone. In a moment, he goes to the kitchen, returns with his tuna plate, and sets it down on the table. He looks with disinterest at his dinner, picks at it with his fingers, then pushes the plate away disgustedly. He violently slams a chair against the table and storms off to the kitchen again. He soon returns with a half gallon of fudge swirl ice cream. He turns on the TV, sits in front of it and eats the ice cream out of its container with a vengeance. Lights fade except for the bluish light of the television which illuminates* HERBIE. MITCHELL *steps out of the darkness to talk to us*)

MITCHELL: There's this scene in my musical that's not in the original. All the Lomans go off on a picnic together to Prospect Park. I thought it would lighten things up a little bit. *You* know, a little up–tempo production number. (*Beat*) Everybody's young and happy. Biff's wearing his varsity T-shirt and he and Happy are tossing around the football, and Linda's setting the picnic table with laminated paper plates and potato salad and coleslaw, and Willy's at the barbecue in a Kiss-the-Cook apron, flipping the franks. He's got the day off for a change, and he sings something like "Oh What a Beautiful Morning," only that's already been done, but you know what I mean. "What a Picnic!" Something like that. And Willy's dead brother Ben is there, and Charley and Bernard from next door. Even the woman from Boston is there, disguised as a park attendant and laughing all the time. (*Beat*) They're all happy. Everybody. And it's very sunny, but not too hot, and there's no wind blowing away the napkins, and no bees or ants, I mean the insect kind, 'cause there are aunts and uncles and cousins and grandparents. . . . It's a perfect day—maybe that's *it:* (*Sings*) "What a perfect day for a picnic!" Yeah, and the whole family sings in harmony, really beautiful, like on the *Sound of Music* record when they sing "How do you solve a problem like Maria?" (*Beat*) You know, this picnic idea I really like. I love picnics. (*Beat*) We never go on any picnics. (*Fade to black.*)

END OF ACT ONE

ACT
TWO

ACT
TWO

Scene One

The suggestion of a room in a fancy catering establishment.
Flocked wallpaper, mirrors, chandeliers, etc. The family is
dressed to the nines, posing for photographs at STEWIE's
bar mitzvah. DORIS's *hair is done up in elaborate curls and*
she proudly wears a chiffon dress with a fur wrap. HERBIE
and the boys are wearing rented tuxedos and yarmulkes;
STEWIE *is also wearing a tallis. Off, in another room, a*
small band plays music like "Sunrise, Sunset."

DORIS (*to us*): Do I look sensational, or what? Huh? Who
would believe I'm the thirty-eight-year-old mother of a
bar mitzvah boy? How can that be? Thirty-eight? Im-
possible. Look at this figure: I still get into my wedding
dress. Oh, this is a great day. This is my coming–out
party. My graduation day. As Stewie becomes a man, I
become a middle–aged lady. Middle–aged lady, ha! I'll
show them middle–aged! I'm not in the least concerned
with getting older.

HERBIE (*to us*): How the hell I'm gonna pay for this I don't
know. I got docked for taking off a Saturday. Saturdays
at the place are our biggest days. (*Flash.* STEWIE *and*
MITCHELL *step aside as* HERBIE *and* DORIS *pose together;*
they face us but talk to one another)

DORIS: It's your kid's bar mitzvah, they'll understand.

HERBIE: I take off enough Saturdays, they could fire me.

DORIS: It's your kid's bar mitzvah! Nobody's gonna fire you!

HERBIE: I don't know, Doris, if I lose my job . . .

DORIS: You're not gonna lose your job! You been there nineteen years!

HERBIE: They fire guys all the time! Dave *Mendelsohn* they fired!

DORIS: He was stealing!

HERBIE: I don't know, Doris . . . (*Flash.* HERBIE *steps aside as* DORIS *poses with* STEWIE, *pinning on his boutonniere*)

DORIS (*to us*): Dan, my hairdresser, came over this morning to do my hair? He *flipped* over me. He wanted to do my eyes like Cleopatra but that's where I draw the line. I don't want to look schmaltzy; I'm a mother. (*Flash*)

STEWIE (*to us*): Thank God that's over. I'm free! No more Hebrew school. No more practicing. No more dreams about getting up there and disgracing myself. No more afternoons with Mr. Shlosh. Today my youth is handed back to me. I can play with my friends after school again. When I come home from school on Monday, I'm gonna celebrate: I'm gonna eat all the chocolate off ev-

58

Christine Baranski *(center)* as Doris with Jonathan Charles Kaplan
(left) as Mitchell and Harry Barandes *(right)* as Stewie.

*All photos of the 1993 Manhattan Theatre Club production
by Martha Swope.*

Christine Baranski *(left)* as Doris with Liz Larsen as Marsha.

Peter Friedman *(left)* as Herbie with Christine Baranski as Doris.

The Loman Family Picnic Company *(from left to right)*:
Christine Baranski, Peter Friedman, Jonathan Charles Kaplan,
Harry Barandes and Liz Larsen.

ery Mallomar, down to the marshmallow, pop it in my mouth, and dunk the cookie part in milk. (*Flash.* DORIS *and* STEWIE *pose dancing*)

DORIS (*to us*): What a party this is gonna be! A hundred and sixty-seven people, including four of STEWIE's closest friends. Sandy Rose and His Orchestra—they're very good; you hear them? A separate rented room for the smorgasbord. Open bar. Swedish meatballs, cocktail franks, bite-sized knishes, little frilly toothpicks to go with them. Roast beef *au jus*. Julienne potatoes. Salad à la Stewie. Fruit–flavored sherbet shaped like fruit. Viennese table with sparklers, make your own non-dairy sundaes. And the linens! A solid mustard–colored tablecloth, topped with lace so the color peeks through. I went for the mustard because I thought it was masculine; *you* know, for Stewie. (*Flash.* MITCHELL *joins them;* DORIS *bends over so that he and* STEWIE *can kiss her cheeks*) And relatives are coming from all over. Jersey. The Island. This is a big event. A lot of these people, the last time I saw them was when I got married. Now they're seeing my son bar mitzvahed. Isn't it beautiful how life goes on? (*Flash.* DORIS *steps aside and* STEWIE *and* MITCHELL *pose shaking hands*)

MITCHELL (*to us*): I could never sing in front of all those people. There must have been five hundred people there! I don't know how I'm gonna do it. I'll never do it as good as Stewie. I'm gonna be a nervous wreck for two years. I wish I were dead.

STEWIE (*to us*): My voice cracked only once, but it sounded like I did it for effect. I brought down the house. (*Flash.* HERBIE *joins his sons. He poses shaking* STEWIE's *hand while* MITCHELL *watches*)

HERBIE (*to us*): *I* never had anything like *this*, I can tell you that. Maybe my mother served a little dairy when we got back from *shul, if* that. I probably went to run deliveries for my father right after. Yeah, that sounds right. (*Flash.* STEWIE *poses reading a prayer book as* HERBIE *and* MITCHELL *look on*)

STEWIE (*to us*): My friend Jeffrey Smolowitz cleared twenty–two hundred dollars at *his* bar mitzvah. And his was smaller than this. I'm gonna buy an electric guitar and an amp, and a bunch of albums. I made a list last week in back of my science notebook. Twenty–two hundred bucks; that's a lot of albums. (*Flash.* DORIS *rejoins the family pose*)

HERBIE (*to us*): She wanted a big party? (*He shrugs*) All right, we'll have a big party. You want tuxedos? We'll rent tuxedos. Then you have to buy *shoes* to go with the tuxedos for me *and* the boys. And a fancy French razor cut, 'cause a regular haircut wouldn't look right with a tux.

DORIS: It just wouldn't.

HERBIE: And a dress for her—all right, it's gorgeous, but still, aren't we going a little overboard here?

DORIS: This is an event. A big deal. There's no cutting corners when you're putting together an event like this. You go all out, or why bother? (*To* STEWIE *and* MITCHELL) Oh, look, boys: people are starting to arrive. I don't believe it, look who's here. You know how I told you about Hitler murdering the Jews?

MITCHELL: Yeah . . . ?

DORIS: Well there's Grandma's Uncle Izzy. The one who died in the war.

STEWIE: Where?

DORIS: The one in the striped pajamas. (*Calls*) Uncle Izzy! Go into the smorgasbord! You must be starving! (*Blows a kiss*) Mwa! Talk to you later! Ess! Ess! (*To* STEWIE *and* MITCHELL) Did you see who he was with? Cousin Rifka.

MITCHELL: Who?

DORIS: Remember I told you boys about the Triangle Factory Fire? Poor thing. (MARSHA *appears and stands beside* DORIS) Boy, they're really coming out for Stewie's bar mitzvah! (*Flash. The family freezes in a tableau.*)

Scene Two

Lights up on the living room. That night. The front door bursts open and STEWIE, *his tallis flying like a cape, runs in, envelopes spilling out of his hands.* MITCHELL *enters after him, picking up the envelopes that have fallen. They laugh wildly.* HERBIE *enters holding an aluminum tray wrapped in foil, followed by* DORIS *carrying a huge flower arrangement. She sets it down.*

DORIS (*in constant, dance–like movement*): I could've danced all night. My feet are swollen but I don't care; I can't feel them, I'm numb.

HERBIE: Take off your shoes.

DORIS: I don't want to. I like being in heels. I like the elevation. Puts me closer to the clouds where my head already is. (*She spins herself around*) What do you think of your old mom now, huh, boys?

MITCHELL: You looked beautiful, Mom. (*Nudges* STEWIE)

STEWIE: You looked beautiful, Mom.

DORIS: Yeah? Thank you.

STEWIE: Okay, here we go!

DORIS: Mitchell, honey? Undo me? (MITCHELL *unzips her dress, which flaps open.* STEWIE *begins to tear open envelopes and read out loud the various gifts*)

STEWIE: Herb and Betty Beckerman!

DORIS: How much?

STEWIE: Twenty–five–dollar check!

MITCHELL and STEWIE: YAYYYY!

DORIS (*to* HERBIE, *during the above*): Is that what we gave them for Kevin? (HERBIE *shrugs*) I think we did.

STEWIE: Tommy and Mary Ann Sorrentino.

DORIS: Yeah . . . ?

STEWIE: Twenty bucks.

DORIS: All right, they don't know from bar mitzvahs.

HERBIE: Gee, I got a stain on my shirt, Doris, you think the tuxedo place'll fine me? Roast beef juice or something.

DORIS (*correcting him*): Roast beef *au jus*. (HERBIE *takes off his jacket and sits in front of the TV with the aluminum tray. He peels off the foil and begins eating chopped liver with his fingers*)

MITCHELL: And the winner is . . . Aunt Reba and Uncle Morris! Fifty–dollar bond!!

MITCHELL and STEWIE: YAYYY!!!

DORIS: Are you writing this down? Write this down. (MITCHELL *does*)

MITCHELL: Should I separate bonds from checks and cash, or add it all together?

DORIS: However you want to do it, sweetheart.

HERBIE: Greatest chopped liver in the world.

STEWIE: Jake and Lillian Frankfurter and Sons, the pigs in the blanket: forty bucks cash.

MITCHELL: Oooo!

DORIS: Acceptable.

STEWIE: Ross and Sylvia Hirsch: twenty–five!

MITCHELL and STEWIE: YAYYY!

DORIS: Typical.

STEWIE: Marvin and Dorothy Klein, twenty–five–dollar check!

MITCHELL and STEWIE: YAYYY!!

DORIS: Was this a party to remember or what?

HERBIE (*meaning the liver*): Oh! Is this good!

DORIS: When the lights went out and they wheeled in the Viennese table . . .

STEWIE (*a la Jerry Lewis telethon*): Come on, folks, keep those checks coming, don't give up now.

DORIS (*to* MITCHELL): Didn't you love those sparklers?

MITCHELL: Uh huh.

DORIS: It was like a roomful of fireworks.

STEWIE: Shelly and Suzy Levine . . .

DORIS: I felt like crying.

STEWIE: Twenty–five dollars! Thank you!!!

DORIS: STEWIE, I'm sorry about the tablecloths, honey.

STEWIE: It's okay I said, Ma . . .

DORIS: I walked into the main ballroom, I almost died: *cranberry* they gave me.

STEWIE: Don't worry about it . . .

HERBIE (*still about the liver*): Mmm!

DORIS (*to* STEWIE): I ordered *mustard* for you. They said they were one short so they had to give me cranberry. I'm sorry, Stewie. I wanted it to be perfect.

STEWIE: I know, I know, it was, it was.

DORIS: Yeah? And what a band, huh?! Didn't you love the band? I can't stop dancing. What range!

STEWIE: "Hava Nageliah" to "Satisfaction."

HERBIE (*still on the liver*): What do they use that makes it taste so good? It's like cake.

STEWIE: Aunt Ida, Uncle Lou and Cousins Jack and Phyllis: fifty–dollar bond! (MITCHELL *and* STEWIE *start to cheer*)

DORIS (*cutting them off*): Is that all? A fifty–dollar bond from two couples?

STEWIE: No?

DORIS: Thirty–seven fifty, that's how much a fifty–dollar bond costs.

MITCHELL: Really? (*The boys look at one another; a beat*)

MITCHELL and STEWIE: Ssssss.

STEWIE (*telethon voice again*): Come on, folks, please, don't be cheap. Go to your wallets, go to your checkbooks, go to your piggy banks and give!

MITCHELL: Look, Jerry, this pledge just came in: Sandy and Murray Schwartzberg of Hicksville. Twenty–five dollars!

STEWIE: Thank you, Sandy and Murray!

DORIS (*mostly to us*): I don't want to sleep tonight. I'll squish my hair. To wake up with flat hair after a day like this would be like dying. I don't want the day to end. I can't believe this is it. You look forward, you plan . . . over a *year* we've been planning this, and before you know it. . . . My life is over. I've got two years till Mitchell's. That's too far to put even a down payment. Now what? What do I do now? (*A beat; She thinks of something*) Thank–you cards! Yes! Table pictures with us posing at every table! Color glossies! What a souvenir!

HERBIE: Stewie? You ever tasted chopped liver like this in your life?

STEWIE: Never. Never in my thirteen years have I tasted liver like that.

HERBIE: I can't stop eating it.

DORIS: Stop eating it.

HERBIE: I can't.

MITCHELL: I've got a subtotal, you want to hear the subtotal?

STEWIE: Drumroll please . . .

MITCHELL: So far, with a bunch of envelopes to go, the subtotal is . . . four hundred and twenty–five dollars!! (MITCHELL *and* STEWIE *cheer, etc.*)

STEWIE: That's beautiful, ladies and gentlemen.

MITCHELL: Wait, this just in: from Grandma Rose.

DORIS: My mother?

MITCHELL: Wow, you are not gonna believe this: two hundred and fifty dollars!

STEWIE and MITCHELL: WOWWWW!!

DORIS: No kidding. How can she afford that?

HERBIE: Have you tried the chopped liver lately?

DORIS: Will you stop with the chopped liver?!

HERBIE: Don't tell me to stop! Who paid for it?!

DORIS: So eat it all up, I don't care! *Don't* stop! You wanted to take it into the place, you won't have any left!

HERBIE: So I'll buy some more!

DORIS: Buy some more! Do what you want! Dance with me, Herbie! Enough with the liver!

HERBIE: I don't *wanna* dance.

DORIS (*pulling him by his arm*): *Dance* with me!

HERBIE: Doris. . . . A whole *day* of this . . .

DORIS: A little foxtrot?! That's gonna kill ya?!

HERBIE (*tugging his arm free*): I don't *wanna* I said . . . (*A beat*)

DORIS (*hurt*): Well, the hell with *you* . . .

HERBIE (*reaching out to her*): Doris . . .

DORIS: The hell with *you* you don't wanna dance with me . . .

MITCHELL: Mommy?

HERBIE: A whole *day* of dancing . . .

DORIS: Who's gonna dance with me? Hm? Hm, Bar Mitzvah Boy? (*She tickles* STEWIE *under his arms; he finds it both pleasurable and annoying*)

STEWIE: Ma–a–a . . . (*More tickling and protesting*)

DORIS: Hm? How about a dance?

STEWIE: Ma–a, st–o–op . . . (*He cackles with laughter;* MITCHELL *looks on with vicarious interest*)

HERBIE: Stewie. . . . Quiet!

STEWIE: *She's* tickling *me!*

DORIS (*stops tickling him*): Nobody'll dance with me!

MITCHELL: I will.

STEWIE: I'm doing something.

DORIS: You're all a bunch of kill–joys.

MITCHELL: Ma, I'll dance. If you want. (*A beat*)

DORIS: Hm?

MITCHELL: I'll dance with you.

DORIS: You, baby?

MITCHELL: If you want.

DORIS: What a sweetheart. You hear that? Mitchell will dance with me.

STEWIE: Good. *You* dance with her. (DORIS *playfully jabs at him*) Hey!

DORIS (*to* MITCHELL): I'd be honored . . . (*She begins to dance with* MITCHELL) Ready? (MITCHELL *nods shyly; while looking down at their feet,* DORIS *leads him in a cha–cha. She occasionally offers words of encouragement ("Good. . . . Watch . . .").* HERBIE *and* STEWIE, *pretending not to care, soon find themselves looking at* MITCHELL *and* DORIS *with growing resentment; their eyes meet for a moment, but they look away in embarrassment.* DORIS *playfully sticks her tongue out at* HERBIE. *Fade out.*)

Scene Three

Later that night. HERBIE *and* STEWIE *are alone in the living room.* HERBIE *has one eye on the TV and the other on* STEWIE *who is looking through his stack of checks. Long pause.* HERBIE *gets up and turns off the TV.*

HERBIE: You made a list?

STEWIE: Mitchell did.

HERBIE: Let's see. (STEWIE *brings him the list*) Very efficient. Look at that. Such a nice handwriting he has, no?

STEWIE: Uh huh.

HERBIE (*squinting at the total*): So, *how* much you got?

STEWIE: Two thousand three hundred and seventy–five.

HERBIE: Wow. Two thousand . . .

STEWIE: Three hundred and seventy–five.

HERBIE: That's a lot of money, twenty–three seventy–five.

STEWIE: I know.

HERBIE: That's *good.*

STEWIE: Yeah. My friend Jeffrey . . .

HERBIE: You did good.

STEWIE: Yeah? Thanks.

HERBIE: Very good. (*Pause*) I'm . . . *proud* of you.

STEWIE: Yeah? (*Pause*) You are?

HERBIE: Twenty–three hundred bucks? Sure. I *am.*

STEWIE: The money?

HERBIE: No, not just the money. The money, sure. But not just the money. Of course not. The money, that's one thing. No, I mean . . . proud. *You* know. (*Pause*)

STEWIE: You were proud? Of me?

HERBIE: Today? Sure.

STEWIE: Yeah?

HERBIE: A father watching his son? Are you kidding? A father watching his son on a day like today? You *feel* things.

STEWIE: You do?

HERBIE: Oh yeah. A man watching his son become a man? That *men* stuff? You *feel* things.

STEWIE: Like what?

HERBIE: I don't know. Your *life.* You feel your whole *life* . . . (*A beat*) I can't explain it.

STEWIE: You feel . . . what.

HERBIE: I can't explain it, I said. One day it'll happen to you. You'll know what I'm talking about, seeing your son.

STEWIE: Proud you said?

HERBIE: Did *I* say that?

STEWIE: Yeah. You said—

HERBIE: I know. That's true. You *do* feel that. You feel other things too. You'll see. A thing like this happening in your life. . . . It's complicated. You *think*. You *wonder*. I'm forty years old—that's no secret; you know how old I am.

STEWIE: Uh huh.

HERBIE: You're forty years old, you're in the middle of things. You can see your life in both directions. You know what I mean? You're standing in the middle of a big field or something, and you look to your left and you see your whole life, everything up till now. You look to your right, and you can see where it ends, the end is in sight. This creates a feeling in you. You wish . . . (*Pause*)

STEWIE: What. (HERBIE *shakes his head "never mind"; a beat*)

HERBIE: So let's *see*. (STEWIE *holds up the stack*) Let me *see*. (STEWIE *flips through the stack*) You're not gonna let me see?

STEWIE: I'm *showing* you.

HERBIE: I want to *see* it, I can't *see* it?

STEWIE: Look.

HERBIE: What are you gonna do with it?

STEWIE: There are things.

HERBIE: Things?

STEWIE: I want.

HERBIE: Twenty–three hundred bucks? What do you want?

STEWIE: I don't know.

HERBIE: What do you *want?* You see yourself *spending* all that money?

STEWIE: Not *all* . . .

HERBIE: What, on records?

STEWIE: I don't know. (*A beat*) I want a guitar.

HERBIE: A guitar.

STEWIE: An electric.

HERBIE: What, so you can blast it? (*A beat.* STEWIE *gathers his things*) All right all right. Not what are you gonna *do* with it, where you gonna *put* it?

STEWIE: I guess in the bank.

HERBIE: How you gonna put it in the bank on a Saturday night? You can't put it in the bank till Monday.

STEWIE (*Over "in the bank till Monday"*): Oh, you mean tonight? Where I'm gonna put it tonight?

HERBIE: Yeah, where you gonna put it, in your *room?*

STEWIE: Yeah.

HERBIE: No you're not.

STEWIE: Why?

HERBIE: That kind of money?

STEWIE: I'll hide it.

HERBIE: From who?

STEWIE: I don't know, *you're* the one who's worried.

HERBIE: I'm not worried. I'm asking. What if something happens to it?

STEWIE: Over the weekend?

HERBIE: Yeah, you never know.

STEWIE: I'll go to the bank Monday morning.

HERBIE: What if you lose it?

STEWIE: On the way to the bank?

HERBIE: Yeah, that too. What if you're mugged?

STEWIE: I won't be mugged.

HERBIE: How do *you* know? You *know* these things? You *know* that if you hide it in your room you won't *misplace* it?

STEWIE: I'll be careful.

HERBIE: You *know* for sure that someone won't break in tonight?

STEWIE: Dad . . .

HERBIE: No, answer me: you *know* this? You *know* that someone won't break in tonight and *steal*—

STEWIE: How they gonna break in? Through the window?

HERBIE: Possibly.

77

STEWIE: We're on the tenth floor!

HERBIE: Big shot! You know everything, hm? (STEWIE *starts to go*) Hey.

STEWIE: What.

HERBIE: Come here.

STEWIE: *What.*

HERBIE: Come *here.* (*They look at one another for a beat.* HERBIE *smiles*) Let me see all that. (*Extends his hand*)

STEWIE: I *did.*

HERBIE: Not like that. (*Pause. Jokingly*) You're really not gonna let me even *touch* it? My God, your own *father* . . . (STEWIE *hesitates, then gives it to him*) Thank you. Jesus, you'd think God knows . . . (*Hefts the stack*) Woww! Feel *that!* That's heavy! Boy!

STEWIE: Yeah. (*His hand is out, awaiting its return*)

HERBIE: So this is what twenty–three hundred bucks feels like.

STEWIE: Uh huh. Now you know.

HERBIE: I don't think I ever in my life held this much money at once. Except for maybe a day's receipts.

STEWIE (*his hand still out*): Uh huh.

HERBIE: You know how many weeks it would take me to make that? *Weeks.* I take home a hundred and fourteen bucks a week. *You* figure it out. One–fourteen. Figure it out; you're smart.

STEWIE: Dad . . .

HERBIE: Figure it *out.* Ten weeks would be what? Eleven–forty. Twenty weeks . . .

STEWIE: Give me.

HERBIE: Twenty weeks is twenty–two–eighty.

STEWIE: Dad . . .

HERBIE: We're talking over twenty weeks. Half a year practically.

STEWIE: I want to go.

HERBIE: Where you *going?*

STEWIE: My *room.*

HERBIE: Tired?

STEWIE: I want to go to my room, yeah.

HERBIE: I can understand you're tired. (*Pause*)

STEWIE: Dad? (STEWIE *extends his hand for the money. Pause; they look at one another for a long time*)

HERBIE: No, son.

STEWIE: *No?*

HERBIE: I'm gonna put it in my drawer.

STEWIE: Why?

HERBIE: It'll be safe there. You know my drawer, I got all my valuables.

STEWIE: Daddy . . .

HERBIE: What, you don't trust me? It'll be safe in my drawer, believe me. Safer in my drawer than under your *pillow.*

STEWIE: I wasn't gonna put it under my pillow . . .

HERBIE: Whatever.

STEWIE: It's my money.

HERBIE: It's not yours.

STEWIE: What do you mean not mine? It's my bar mitz-vah! All the cards say my name!

HERBIE: I mean it's not yours to *spend.*

STEWIE (*goes through discarded envelopes*): "For Stewie," "For Stewart on his bar mitzvah."

HERBIE (*overlap*): I know, I know. I mean it's not *your* money, it's *our* money.

STEWIE: How is it ours? It's my bar mitzvah!

HERBIE: What we have to do: sign the checks and I'll countersign them.

STEWIE: *How is it ours?*

HERBIE: You're a minor. A kid.

STEWIE: Today I am a man! You even said!

HERBIE: You don't understand something, son.

STEWIE: No, I understand.

HERBIE: We got a misunderstanding.

STEWIE: YOU'RE TAKING MY MONEY!

HERBIE: Oh, shut up. Who the hell you think is *paying* for this thing? Hm? You think Rockefeller? (MITCHELL, *in his pajamas, watches from the foyer*)

STEWIE: I thought *you.*

HERBIE: *Me?* With *what?*

STEWIE: I don't know. *You're* the father.

HERBIE: With what am I supposed to be paying for this with? Hm? Do I have the money for this kind of thing?

STEWIE: I don't know.

HERBIE: How would I have that kind of money? Schmuck. Think about it: I told you what I take home.

STEWIE: Yeah . . .

HERBIE: So where am I getting the money to throw *you* a fancy party? (STEWIE *shrugs. A beat*) The gifts!

STEWIE: You mean with the *gifts?*

HERBIE: Yeah. That's how we have to do it: what comes in has to go right out again. Didn't you *know* that?

STEWIE: No.

HERBIE: What, you thought I was gonna shell out all this money, to make you a party, just shell it all out of the kindness of my heart? Is that what you thought?

STEWIE: I didn't think, I don't know.

HERBIE: Look at this bill. (*Takes it from his jacket pocket*) No, look at it. Thirty-two hundred sixty-four dollars and twenty-two cents. That's what just today cost. 32–64–22. Do you know what kind of money that is? And that doesn't count the hundred-buck deposit we had to put down a year ago, and your mother's dress, and these special suits we rented, and the photographer taking colored pictures. *And* the flowers. *And* the so–and–so. The *band.* We're talking four grand here. Four grand! You think your father has four thousand dollars? Where have you *been?* This is what I been trying to tell you! The gifts are only gonna cover half! I'm two grand in the hole! Even *with* your precious gifts! Two grand in the hole!

STEWIE: I'll loan you some. You can borrow.

HERBIE: You're telling *me?!* You're telling *me* I can *borrow?!* Who's the father here?! Hm? Who pays the bills around here? Who hands out your allowance?! You don't tell *me* I can *borrow!*

STEWIE: Why didn't you tell me this before?! Why didn't you tell me I'd have to pay for my own bar mitzvah?!

HERBIE: Why didn't I *tell* you? I thought you'd figure it out for yourself.

STEWIE: So why did we do this? I didn't want it.

HERBIE: Why did we *do* this? Everybody does it.

STEWIE: My friend Jeffrey . . .

HERBIE: How would it look if we didn't throw you a bar mitzvah?

STEWIE: I don't know.

HERBIE: It would look very funny. Like something was wrong.

STEWIE: Isn't something wrong?

HERBIE: Hm?

STEWIE: You mean it would've looked like we couldn't afford it, so you made one anyway, even though we couldn't afford it!

HERBIE: Don't open a mouth like that to me.

STEWIE: But isn't it true?

HERBIE: Don't open a mouth.

STEWIE (*overlap*): We couldn't afford it. Say it. We couldn't afford it but you did it anyway and *I* have to pay for something I didn't even ask for in the first place!

HERBIE (*enraged, he shakes* STEWIE *violently*): YOU THINK I WANT YOUR MONEY?!!

MITCHELL (*approaches timidly*): Daddy . . .

HERBIE (*to* MITCHELL): Get outta here. (*To* STEWIE, *while shaking him*) YOU THINK I LIKE HAVING TO DO THIS?!!

DORIS (*calls from off–stage*): I hear body–drops in there!

STEWIE (*overlap*): YOU MADE A MISTAKE AND *I* HAVE TO PAY FOR IT!

MITCHELL: Daddy, stop . . .

HERBIE (*to* MITCHELL): Get *away* I said.

STEWIE (*overlap*): WHY SHOULD I HAVE TO PAY FOR YOUR MISTAKES? IT ISN'T FAIR!—

DORIS (*off*): I hear body–drops!

STEWIE: —I'M JUST A KID!

HERBIE: UH! *NOW* YOU'RE A KID! *NOW* YOU'RE A KID!

MITCHELL (*tugging on* HERBIE): Daddy . . .

HERBIE (*to* MITCHELL): I TOLD YOU—(*Pushes him*)

STEWIE (*adrenalin rushing madly*): HEY! DON'T YOU TOUCH *HIM*. YOU HEAR ME? (*Swipes at* HERBIE *with his fist*) DON'T YOU TOUCH MY BROTHER!

HERBIE: YOU WANT TO FIGHT? HM? YOU WANT TO KILL ME? (STEWIE *and* HERBIE *are throwing punches;* DORIS *comes in*)

DORIS: Boys! What the—Herbie! Stop that!

HERBIE (*still sparring*): I should stop?! He started!

DORIS: Herbie! What's the matter with you?!

STEWIE (*throwing punches; nearly hysterical*): HE HATES US, MOMMY! HE HATES US!

HERBIE (*that did it; he's going berserk*): YOU THINK I DON'T LOVE YOU?!! YOU THINK I DON'T *LOVE* YOU?!! (DORIS *puts her arms protectively around the shaken boys*)

DORIS: Herbie, shush! The house is shaking!

HERBIE (*jabbing at* STEWIE): I DON'T LOVE YOU?!!

DORIS (*shielding* STEWIE): DON'T HURT HIM!

HERBIE: LOOK AT YOU WITH YOUR PRECIOUS BOYS! WHAT DO *I* GET, HM?! (*Storms off to bedroom, screaming*) WHAT DO *I* HAVE! WHAT DO *I* HAVE! (DORIS *has her arms around both whimpering boys when* HERBIE *returns carrying a dresser drawer. Now at a terrifying pitch*) EVERYTHING I HAVE IS HERE IN THIS DRAWER! EVERYTHING I OWN

IS RIGHT HERE! I COULD GET THE HELL OUT
OF HERE LIKE *THAT!*

DORIS: Herbie, shhh . . .

HERBIE (*overlap*): WHAT DO I *HAVE?!* WHAT'S *MINE?!*
THIS MUCH SPACE IN THE CLOSET?! One suit?!
You can *keep* the suit; I don't give a damn about that
suit; I hate suits; you made me buy that suit.

DORIS (*quietly*): I thought you needed—

HERBIE: DONATE IT TO GOODWILL! MAKE BE-
LIEVE I DIED! WEAR IT FOR HALLOWEEN!
WHAT DO I *HAVE!* I HAVE NOTHING! I HAVE
SHIT! I HAVE THE TOILET FOR TEN MINUTES
IN THE MORNING! I DON'T EVEN HAVE *YOU!*

DORIS: Herbie . . .

HERBIE: LOOK AT YOU! LOOK WHO GETS *YOU!*

DORIS: That's not true—the boys . . .

HERBIE (*overlap*): WHAT DO *I* HAVE! I DON'T EVEN
HAVE THE TV! KEEP THE TV! THE HELL WITH
THE TV! I'll buy myself a *new* TV. Top of the line!
Color! Yeah, I'll buy myself a *color!* The boys can have
the old one, watch whatever the hell they want! WHAT
DO *I* GET?! WHAT DOES *DADDY* GET? (*Shaking
the drawer violently*) EVERYTHING IN THE

WORLD THAT'S MINE IS RIGHT HERE IN THIS
DRAWER! EVERYTHING! What do I have? Underwear? This underwear is shot. Do I buy myself any? Do
I buy myself anything? Look at these socks! Holes!
Holes burned through 'em but I wear 'em anyway, tear-
ing up my feet! My feet are torn up! Do I go to a foot
doctor?! Look at all these single, lost socks I hold onto
hoping the other'll show up! Look at this! The hell with
them! Garbage! LOOK AROUND THIS HOUSE!
WHAT'S MINE?! NOTHING! (*Rummaging through
the drawer*) I got my coin collection! My silver dollars!
What am I? Cufflinks? Tie clips? Skins? Undershorts
with shot elastic? T–shirts with holes under the arms?
THIS IS ME?! THIS IS MY LIFE! THIS DRAWER
IS MY WHOLE LIFE, RIGHT HERE; THIS
DRAWER! (*He throws the drawer down and storms out
of the apartment*)

DORIS: HERBIE! (*A sudden burst of music punctuates the
action, signalling the start of a musical number.* MITCH-
ELL *is alone. The following lines in caps. are all sung*)

MITCHELL:
HEY, WHY DON'T WE
GET AWAY FROM ALL THIS?
WE ALL COULD USE A LITTLE
CHANGE OF SCENE.
LET'S GO SOMEWHERE
A LITTLE GREEN IN PLACES,
WHERE A LITTLE BREATHING SPACE IS,
AND THE AIR IS CLEAN.

LET'S GO
WHERE WE CAN SHOW
OFF OUR SUNGLASSES.
YEAH, LET ME TAKE YOU ALL
TO WHERE THE GRASS IS!

(*With the tempo change, painted scenery moves in and lighting shifts*)

WHAT A PERFECT DAY
FOR A PICNIC!
WE'LL TOAST MARSHMALLOWS
IN THE SUN!

WHAT A PERFECT DAY
FOR A FAM'LY PICNIC!
ROASTING CHICKEN,
HAVING FUN!

STASH THE SLINKY!
PACK PARCHEESI!
FILL THE FOOTBALL
UP WITH AIR!
WE'LL PLAY CATCH IN THE PARK
TILL IT STARTS TO GET DARK,
AND TAKE MEM'RIES HOME TO SHARE!

(*As* MITCHELL *sings the following,* STEWIE *enters broodingly, wearing a yarmulke, a varsity sweater over his tuxedo and reading his Haftarah booklet.* MITCHELL *tries to get his attention*)

IT'S A PERFECT DAY
FOR A PICNIC!
FOR THE SKY WOULDN'T DARE TURN GRAY!
WHAT DO YOU SAY, BROTHER?
LET'S GET AWAY, BROTHER.
STEWIE, WHAT DO YOU SAY?
WHAT DO YOU SAY, BROTHER?
WE'RE ON OUR WAY, BROTHER!
STEWIE, LET'S ALL GO OUT AND—

STEWIE:

WHAT IS IT THAT I DO?
IT'S NOTHING I CAN NAME.
IT DOESN'T MATTER WHAT I DO,
IT'S MY FAULT ALL THE SAME.

MITCHELL:

A PICNIC!
A PICNIC, STEWIE!

STEWIE:

WHAT IS IT THAT I SAY
THAT MAKES ME FEEL ASHAMED?
IT DOESN'T MATTER WHAT I SAY,
I KNOW THAT I'M TO BLAME.

MITCHELL:

A PICNIC!
THINK PICNIC, STEWIE!
THINK SUNSHINE!

STEWIE:

IT'S ALWAYS SOMETHING.
IT'S ALWAYS SOMETHING.

(*A little soft–shoe*)

SOMETHING FUNNY'S GOING ON.
SOMETHING FUNNY WITH OUR DAD.
I DON'T MEAN SOMETHING FUNNY HA–HA,
I MEAN IT'S SOMETHING FUNNY–SAD.

MITCHELL: There's nothing we can do about it, Stewie. Nothing. (*During the following,* MITCHELL *follows* STEWIE's *steps and dances with him*)

STEWIE:

DAD'S A LITTLE WEIRD,
HE'S IN A DAZE.
COULD IT BE HE'S GOING NUTS?
OR IS IT JUST A PHASE?

MITCHELL:

YOU'RE RIGHT.
DAD'S WEIRD.

STEWIE:

DAD'S A LITTLE OFF,
HE'S FEELING PAIN.
IS IT THAT HE'S OVERWORKED
OR JUST A BIT INSANE?
HE'S STRANGE.

MITCHELL: DAD'S STRANGE.

STEWIE: SOMETHING FUNNY'S GOING ON.

MITCHELL: SOMETHING FUNNY'S GOING ON.

STEWIE: SOMETHING FUNNY WITH OUR DAD.

MITCHELL: SOMETHING FUNNY WITH OUR DAD.

STEWIE and MITCHELL:
I DON'T MEAN SOMETHING FUNNY HA–HA,
I MEAN IT'S SOMETHING FUNNY–SAD.

(DORIS *enters*)

DORIS:
ATTENTION!
ATTENTION!
YOU MUST PAY ATTENTION
TO SUCH A MAN AS YOUR DAD.
IN HIS SOUL I KNOW WHERE
EV'RY NOOK AND CRANNY IS.
YOU JUST DON'T UNDERSTAND
THE SORT OF MAN
HE IS.

HE'S NOT A BAD MAN
HE'S NOT A GREAT MAN.
YES, HE MAY EVEN BE A TRULY
SECOND–RATE MAN.

CALL HIM GOOD, CALL HIM BAD,
THAT'S JUST FINE—
HE'S MINE.

HE'S NOT A KIND MAN,
BUT—NOT A MEAN MAN.
GUESS YOU COULD SAY
HE'S JUST YOUR AVERAGE
IN–BETWEEN MAN.
I DON'T CARE, I DON'T CRY,
I DON'T WHINE—
HE'S MINE!

HE'S NOT A LOSER.
HE'S NOT A WINNER.
AND, YES, I WISH HE WERE
A LITTLE THINNER.
OR MAYBE ONCE A WEEK
GET HOME FOR DINNER
BEFORE NINE.

HE'S NOT A DREAMBOAT,
NO CASANOVA.
BUT HE WILL BE MY MAN
UNTIL MY LIFE IS OVER.
AM I RIGHT? AM I WRONG?
AM I BLIND?
HE'S MINE!

DON'T MOCK HIM, MITCHELL!
DON'T SNICKER, STEWIE!

FOR THOUGH YOU MAY BELIEVE
HE'S DULL, OR DUMB, OR SCREWY,
WHEN HE WALKS THROUGH THAT DOOR,
IT'S A SIGN—
HE'S MINE!

(*The front door opens and* HERBIE *enters wearily in a hat and overcoat, carrying two large valises*)

DORIS: Herbie!

HERBIE: Oy!

MITCHELL and STEWIE: Dad!

HERBIE: Ugh!
YOU SHOULDA SEEN ME TODAY, BOYS!
I WAS CLEVER! I WAS QUICK!
THE WORLD WAS GOING MY WAY, BOYS!
I WAS LIGHTNING! I WAS SLICK!
BOY, WAS I HOT, BOYS!
BOY, WAS I BRIGHT!
BRIGHT AS ANY SHOOTING STAR
THAT LIGHTS UP THE NIGHT!
YOU SHOULDA SEEN HOW I HANDLED THE
    CROWD—
IF YOU'DA SEEN ME TODAY, BOYS,
YOU WOULDA BEEN PROUD!

(MITCHELL *throws him an umbrella and he uses it as a*

song–and–dance man would a cane. His routine becomes
more and more frantic)

YOU SHOULDA SEEN ME
ANSWERING CALLS,
ORDER AFTER ORDER,
TILL I'M BOUNCING OFF WALLS.

YOU SHOULDA SEEN ME
GOING FOR BROKE,
SHAKING ALL THOSE CLAMMY
HANDS AND CRACKING BAD JOKES.

YOU SHOULDA SEEN ME
FAKING AND LYING
SHPIELING AND DEALING,
NOBODY BUYING.
SCHMOOZING AND LOSING
NEVER STOPPED TRYING.
FRETTING AND SLIPPING
AND SWEATING AND SCHLEPPING
AND YELLING AND CRYING
BUT KNOWING I'M DYING.
(*he collapses*) I'm dead . . .

DORIS (*goes to him*):
GIVE ME YOUR FEET,
I'LL RUB THEM.
TAKE OFF YOUR SOCKS AND SHOES.
HAND ME YOUR FEET, I'LL SCRUB THEM
I'LL SCRUB AWAY YOUR BLUES

I KNOW YOUR SOLES ARE HURTING
I KNOW YOUR SOUL CAN SING!

ALL (*including* MARSHA, *who has entered during the above*): AHHHH!

DORIS:
PUT YOUR FEET IN MY HANDS,
OH THEY'RE SWEET IN MY HANDS,
PUT YOUR FEET IN MY HANDS,
WITH YOUR FEET IN MY HANDS,
YOU'LL NEVER WALK ALONE!

ALL (*variously; with great urgency*):
SEEMS TO ME IT'S TIME
FOR A PICNIC!
WE CAN STILL GET OUR SHARE OF SUN.
WHAT A PERFECT DAY
FOR A FAMILY PICNIC!

PLAYING MAHJ–JONGG,
HAVING FUN!
FOLD THE CHAIRS UP!
PACK THE PEANUTS!
FILL THE ICE CHEST
WITH DRY ICE!
YOU CAN NAP IN THE SHADE,
MAYBE DRINK LEMONADE—
IT'S A STEAL AT ANY PRICE!

(*Thunder.* HERBIE, STEWIE, DORIS *and* MARSHA *exit*)

MITCHELL:
IT WAS A PERFECT DAY
FOR A PICNIC,
TILL THE CLOUDS MADE THE SKY TURN
   DARK.
THERE'LL BE ANOTHER DAY
WE'LL HAVE OUR CHANCE TO PLAY.
HEY, FOLKS, WHAT DO YOU SAY?
MAYBE SOME OTHER DAY
I'LL TAKE US ALL AWAY
TO A PICNIC
IN THE
PARK!

(*The scenery disappears. Fade out.*)

Scene Four

Late that night. DORIS *paces fretfully.* MARSHA *lights two cigarettes* Now, Voyager *style.*

DORIS: I saw this movie. Pure Lana Turner, I know. But this is what's happened to my life, Marsh. My life is a B–movie. (MARSHA *hands her a cigarette*) Thanks. I don't know what to do.

MARSHA: You gotta leave the bum.

DORIS: He's not a bum, Marsh, don't call him a bum.

MARSHA: Bum or no, you gotta leave him.

DORIS: How?

MARSHA: One foot in front of the other.

DORIS: Just like that? How? How do I do that?

MARSHA: Look, you said yourself: the guy's lost his marbles.

DORIS: Completely. Yes. You should have seen him. The way he shook—

MARSHA: So what's the problem? Kiddo, this is your life, too. Take it from me. Time is short. It's rare, too good to waste on a dead–end proposition and that's what you got here.

DORIS: Oh, but, Marsh, people where we come from, it's unheard of. You know that. You of all people should. Jewish people don't go their separate ways, they stick it out even if they're miserable. We're like Catholics that way. Only I'm not worried about the Pope excommunicating me; my *mother* will sit *shiva* for me. She'll cover the mirrors and sit close to the ground. I'll call her on the phone and say, "Ma, it's me, your daughter, Doris," and she'll say, "My daughter Doris is dead" and hang up.

MARSHA: You gotta break out, kiddo. Grab your little boys and walk into the sunset. You gotta do it, Doll. If not you, send him out on his can. The party's over. You can do it. You gotta. (*A key turns in the front door*)

DORIS: Marsha, please, I . . .

MARSHA: You gotta, kid. It's the only way. (MARSHA *exits as* HERBIE *enters through the front door. He and* DORIS *look at one another for a long beat before he speaks*)

HERBIE: I went to the movies. Anything. *Born Free.* The lions. Africa. Lots of growling, jumping around the fields. About lions yearning to breathe free or something. Dumb picture. I fell asleep. (DORIS *gets up*) Don't worry about my supper. I ate Bon Bons.

DORIS: Herbie.

HERBIE (*a beat*): Yeah?

DORIS (*a beat*): This is it, Herbie.

HERBIE (*a beat; a nervous smile*): Wha?

DORIS: I don't care anymore, Herbie. I can't be the good little girl anymore, the good daughter, the good wife. I can't live like this anymore, Herbie, the silence is deafening. I'm bored, Herbie, I'm dying. What am I saying? I hear myself talk and I can't believe how Harold Robbins I sound. I married for life, I know. I bought the whole *megillah:* love, honor, protect, till death. But I take it all back. Sorry for the inconvenience. They should have you take the vow: I'll love you forever or till I'm all used up, whichever comes first. I'm used *up* all right, Herbie, like a tube a toothpaste all squeezed out, but you don't stop squeezing. We've become one of those couples we'd see in restaurants, who go through a whole meal and don't say a word to each other.

HERBIE: We're talking now.

DORIS: Me. *I'm* talking. I do all the talking for both of us. I do all the thinking. It's gotten so I don't bother to say anything 'cause I know your half of the conversation.

HERBIE: Isn't that good? Isn't that knowing a person so well . . .

DORIS: No, it's just knowing the other half of the conversation. I'm very sorry, Herbie. You're a sweet man. You'll find someone. I'm used up. I can't prop you up and make you feel good when you should feel lousy. I can't cover for you and make excuses. I can't run your public relations anymore, Herbie. Eighteen years; that's not so bad. Nothing to be ashamed of. Who *says* you have to be married to just one person your whole life? Yeah, at this rate you still have time to squeeze in another couple eighteen–year marriages. You and the *next* eighteen–year lady, the two of you'll have a great time, I promise, Herbie. She'll either pick up where I left off and be your mother all over again or, if you're lucky.

. . . (*A beat*) I can't make up for your childhood anymore. And neither can the boys. I'm sorry, my job is
done. I quit. (*A beat*) I packed up your drawer in the
American Tourister like I'm sending you off to camp for
the last time. Kiss the boys goodbye. We'll be in touch.
(*Lighting shifts.* DORIS *and* HERBIE *resume their places at
the top of the scene and begin it again*)

HERBIE: I went to the movies. *Born Free*. The lions. Africa.
About lions yearning to breathe free or something.
Dumb picture. I fell asleep. (DORIS *gets up*) Don't worry
about my supper. I ate Bon Bons.

DORIS: Herbie. (*A beat*)

HERBIE: Yeah? (*A beat*)

DORIS: This is it, Herbie. (*A beat*)

HERBIE (*a nervous smile*): Wha?

DORIS: My life is over, but it's still going on. I always
wanted to go down in a blaze of glory, young and beautiful like my Aunt Marsha. What tragedy! What drama!
Frozen gorgeous. Never forgotten. Never old. All that
promise, all that youth, wasted. People never stop won-
dering what might've been. Forever twenty–three. Not
bad. I want to be frozen in your mind, forever thirty–
eight. (*A beat*) My life is over, Herbie. I have the boys,
but I don't have them; they won't be mine much
longer. They'll survive; children do. Children never re-

101

member the good stuff anyway, they only remember the shit. My life is over, stop the projector. It's the going *on* that's painful, not the going. There's no place left for me to go. We worked so hard to get to where we are, Herbie, to this luxury, but this is as far as they'll let us go. This is it for us: The top, the last stop. We have arrived. I'm stuck, Herbie. I'm stuck up here on the tenth floor. There's nowhere to go but out the window. Goodbye, Herbie. Kiss the boys goodbye. (*She opens the door to the terrace, puts one foot over the railing and jumps. Lighting shifts.* DORIS *and* HERBIE *resume their places at the top of the scene and begin it again*)

HERBIE: I went to the movies. *Born Free.* About lions yearning to breathe free or something. Dumb picture. I fell asleep. (DORIS *gets up*) Don't worry about my supper. I ate Bon Bons.

DORIS: Herbie. (*A beat*)

HERBIE: Yeah?

DORIS (*Runs into his arms; tearfully*): Don't ever run out on me like that again, you hear me?! I never felt so lonely in my life! How dare you do that to me?! When I married you I thought, here is a man who'll never leave me, and when you did, it was like a part of me was stolen, my leg, my child. I need you to take care of. Who'm I gonna take care of if you leave me? The boys need me less and less; what happens when they don't need me at all? I need you, Herbie. Don't let me go.

Please don't let me go. (HERBIE *sways with* DORIS *in his arms. He gently sings the first verse of "Autumn Leaves."* MITCHELL *and* STEWIE *run out of their room*)

STEWIE and MITCHELL: Daddy! Daddy! (*Etc. They embrace* HERBIE. *Lighting shifts. The boys exit.* DORIS *and* HERBIE *resume their places at the top of the scene and begin it again*)

HERBIE: I went to the movies. Anything. *Born Free.* The lions. Africa. Lots of growling, jumping around fields. About lions yearning to breathe free or something. Dumb picture. I fell asleep. (DORIS *makes a move*) Don't worry about my supper. I ate Bon Bons.

DORIS: Bon Bons? That's why I bust my chops making you Weight Watchers? I made you a tuna plate for when you got home. Eat it and eliminate your fruit today and tomorrow. Bon Bons! (*As she goes to the kitchen*) Sit. (HERBIE *does;* DORIS *returns with his tuna plate, sets it down in front of him, and sits beside him as he begins to eat.* MITCHELL *watches them. Finally,* HERBIE *speaks*)

HERBIE (*sheepishly*): Doris, look, I'm sorry about—

DORIS: Don't. (*A beat. Quietly*) Don't. (*A beat.* HERBIE *resumes eating, and* DORIS *watches him in silence, as the lights fade very slowly.*)

END OF PLAY